AT LAST YOU WIN

By Luang Por Dhammajayo

To:

_____

_____

From:

_____

At Last You Win
By Luang Por Dhammajayo

Copyrighted by *Dhammakaya Foundation*
40 Mu 8, Khlong Song, Khlong Luang District,
Pathum Thani Province, Thailand 10120
www.dhammakaya.net

Download E-Book Version at: www.tawandhamma.org

Designed by Beamers Net Pte Ltd.
            DM&S Advertising Co.Ltd.

ISBN: 978-616-7200-15-6

PREFACE

Dhammakaya Foundation
1 January 2011

"Laypeople always worry about obstacles, but there are extraordinary people for whom overcoming them is child's play."

Our lives are always challenged by competitions and rivalries in which we are obliged to participate for expected achievement, whether they are significant or insignificant. As a result, there are numerous barriers and goals on the path of our journey through life. This certainly consumes our physical and mental energy. In order to overcome these obstacles before they overwhelm us, we must strengthen ourselves from within.

When it comes to physical strength, we know that we must eat nutritious and wholesome food and also exercise to have a strong, healthy and functional body. However, most people do not know how to fortify their mental health. Some of the physically strongest people may still find themselves overcome by challenges in their lives.

This book is a collection of powerful words of wisdom from Luang Por Dhammajayo (The Most Venerable Dhammajayo Bhikkhu) spoken during his sermons. It aims to reveal the secrets of developing and maintaining a strong and stable mind.

Whenever you feel discouraged, weary and hopeless from the crushing waves of life, the advice and encouragement in this book can be your lighthouse. Its recommendations can relieve your mental weariness, cheer you up, and help you to achieve your life's goals. In the end, it is up to you to overcome any challenges.

I.THE WORLD'S COMMON PROBLEMS

II. CONFRONTING OBSTACLES

III. SOLUTIONS FROM WISDOM

IV. THE WAY OF SOLITUDE

V. ABOVE ALL CIRCUMSTANCES

VI. THE POWER OF THE MIND

VII. THE TRUE REFUGE

THE WORLD'S COMMON PROBLEMS

I

The Eight Worldly Conditions

The eight things associated
with worldly life are gain and loss;
honour and dishonour;
happiness and misery; and praise and blame.
All of these are inevitable for everyone,
whether they are willing to face it or not.
Whenever good karma bears fruit
one will receive gain, honour, happiness, and
praise. On the contrary, when bad karma has its
effect, one suffers from loss, dishonour, misery,
and blame. Everyone who lives the worldly life
will encounter these conditions
because this world is ruled
by the Law of Karma.

29 July 2002

THE WORLD'S COMMON PROBLEMS

II

The World of Defiled Minds

1 July 2007

Irrespective of the prevailing
situation, we have to accept all
happenings as the way of the world.
Common people are subject to
mental impurities in various degrees,
and while some are able to liberate
themselves from defilement,
many people live aimlessly.

This is because the truth of life is unknown to them. Thus, it is important to maintain the quality of your mind. Do not let trouble disturb your heart. No matter what problems you come across, handle them wisely.

28 July 2007

We must learn to let go, forgive and share loving kindness with each other because we all have defilements and are affected by the Eight Worldly Conditions (Lokadhamma). The ups and downs of life occur due to the karma from our past deeds. For example, when the merit from generosity gives results, we are rewarded with gains.

THE WORLD'S COMMON PROBLEMS III

Improve Oneself First

When the merit is exhausted, our gains will vanish. This is also true for honour, fame and happiness.

So why waste our time trying to correct others? Instead, we should focus on improving ourselves first. Once we can fix our own flaws our lives will become much happier.

THE WORLD'S COMMON PROBLEMS

IV

Stronger Defilement Leads To Weaker Wisdom

This world is a gathering place of imperfect people. Both men and women have a dark side to their minds. The springing up of mental impurity always taints one's mind, leading to weaker wisdom and stronger craving. Fortunately, stillness from meditation allows us to enjoy peace and happiness that stem from within; and our minds will become firm, stable and indifferent towards misery.

4 June 2007

THE WORLD'S COMMON PROBLEMS
V
Separation is Normal

Separation from the things we love is normal. This applies not only to our belongings, property and home, but also our own bodies. No matter how hard we try, it is impossible to keep them with us forever.

15 September 2006

For example, as we grow older, we lose our teeth or our hair against our will. Eventually, youth and beauty fade away because they do not really belong to us permanently. We own them only temporarily. Thus, separation is certain to come. If it is not us who die first and leave all these things behind, then we are the one who witness the loss of people and things. That is the way of life.

THE WORLD'S COMMON PROBLEMS

VI

Suffering is Universal

Most people do not get what they want. Even their own spouse, who they expect to spend their whole life with, sometimes turns out to be the wrong choice. Everyone has had unpleasant experiences with living and non-living things, and sometimes we are deprived of the things we cherish.

Thus mental suffering, which is a universality of life, exists for those who experience disappointment and dissatisfaction. The Lord Buddha introduced a solution to this condition, thus allowing his followers to be enlightened and joyous at last. After attaining inner wisdom, one will rise from the illusionary world and achieve bliss within oneself.

22 December 2006

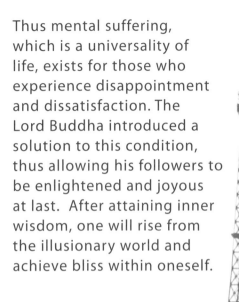

THE WORLD'S COMMON PROBLEMS VII

End the Cycle of Rebirth

Death, a normal occurrence, is a process in which we are transferred from one body to another. The Lord Buddha affirmed that death causes suffering when it separates us from the people we love.

Therefore, He suggested that there should be no death in this world. This can only happen if we end the process of rebirth by following the methods that He discovered.

We need to learn how to prepare ourselves for death so that we are able to attain Nirvana and put an end to the process of rebirth.

6 November 2006

THE WORLD'S COMMON PROBLEMS VIII

No Fear of Death

There is no pain greater than the pain from death. When one is dying, one might be overwhelmed with severe pain. It could be so strong that one prefers to leave the physical body right away. All other forms of suffering seem to pale in comparison. In order to cope with death, we must learn to be fully conscious and remain calm while facing pain and suffering. Please remember that darkness does not last forever. The night will eventually be replaced by the dawn of a new day.

23 June 2007

Death may visit us at anytime. It is certain that everybody has to die, without knowing in advance exactly where, when and why. We should be aware that death is waiting for us, and we should take time to practice meditation without any excuses.

THE WORLD'S COMMON PROBLEMS IX

Death is Certain

28 September 2003

Blaming your problems on someone or something is never a good excuse since obstacles occur when our merit energy is weak.

Moreover, without merit from meditation practice, we lack the positive energy for lessening or removing our obstructions in life.

THE WORLD'S COMMON PROBLEMS

X

Do Not Be Reckless

3 June 2007

When contemplating the reality of all animate and inanimate things like humans, animals, trees, mountains, buildings or the earth itself, we all share the same cycle. Everything is destined to take its shape, last for a while and then perish. This is the same as our ancestors who have gone before us. There is no exception even with the past Buddhas who possessed supreme insight, knowledge and superb conduct. They had to leave their physical form and enter Nirvana. We too, one day will have to leave this world. This cycle of death and rebirth has repeated itself over and over innumerable lifetimes. Once we are aware of this fact, we should learn how to relinquish all ephemeral things. The rest of our lives should be devoted to the true purpose of human birth. Do not be reckless by allowing yourself to be carried away with worldly pleasures.

Have a close look at this world. Utilize your possessions including life, wealth, family, friends, intelligence, wisdom and power, to perform good deeds and pursue perfections. We should keep this in mind every day. Do not delay yourself any further as it might be too late, for death may snatch you away without warning. Then we lose everything we have, and there is no opportunity to perform good deeds anymore.

CONFRONTING
OBSTACLES
XI
The World of Problems

All the countries in this world are burdened with problems at one time or another. Problems are everywhere -starting with ourselves, our family, neighborhood, city, province, country, and the international community. Problems exist regardless of social class; whether one is poor, middle class, or elite. Each class has its own unique problems, to a greater or lesser degree, whether one is a billionaire or a beggar.

29 July 2002

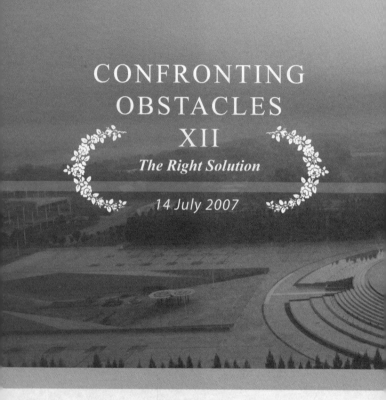

CONFRONTING OBSTACLES

XII

The Right Solution

14 July 2007

People have to face problems at every stage of life whether they are children, adolescents, teenagers, adults, or elders. Nobody can escape from problems which arrive in many forms. As one has to grow, it is necessary to prepare to confront these problems.

Since the knowledge we learned at school could be too limited to produce effective solutions, we must learn more from the Lord Buddha's knowhow in order to solve problems in this world righteously and successfully.

CONFRONTING OBSTACLES XIII

Solvable and Insolvable

26 September 2002

According to the Lord Buddha, there are two types of problems: *satekiccha* and *atekiccha*, which means solvable and insolvable. This denotes that not every problem can be solved. For example, when we accidentally cut our finger, the wound will heal. However, if we are beheaded, there is no way to bring us back to life. When encountering an insolvable problem, the best we can do is to remain calm and peaceful. We should not let our mind suffer any further.

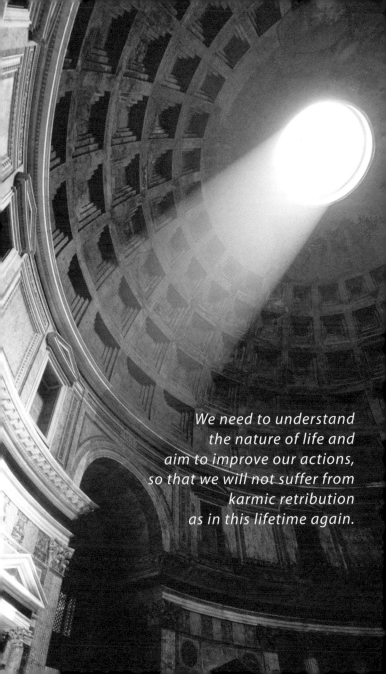

*We need to understand
the nature of life and
aim to improve our actions,
so that we will not suffer from
karmic retribution
as in this lifetime again.*

CONFRONTING
OBSTACLES
XIV

Knowledge for the Crisis

As we age with the ebb and flow of time in this world, our understanding about life becomes more mature. We must understand that *Dhamma* is very beneficial when we are faced with difficulties in life. Thus, we should acquire this knowledge in good time, so that in times of crisis we will not be left devastated and not knowing what to do.

14 July 2007

CONFRONTING OBSTACLES
XV
A Compass for Life

In our daily lives, we cannot be guided by professional knowledge alone. We also need Dhamma to guide us towards the right livelihood. In this way, whenever we confront an obstacle, we can reassure ourselves and overcome it wisely.

30 June 2007

CONFRONTING OBSTACLES
XVI

Handling Obstacles

Every obstacle exists to be overcome. Similar to the waves that beautify the sea, obstacles enrich our life experience. If we run down to the sea with our surfboard and find no waves, we will miss the fun and excitement. Likewise, the sea of life requires obstacles to challenge and test our strength.

23 February 2008

We need to keep our mind still at the center of the body, in the same manner that we keep our body balanced on the surfboard. Our mind should be indifferent towards people, things and issues that exacerbate problems. We can train our mind daily to be stable and subtle by stilling it through meditation.

CONFRONTING OBSTACLES
XVII
Peace of Mind

Life is not always smooth-sailing and we do not always know what lies in store for us. Whenever we have difficulties, we should not retreat or suffer from remorse. We can lose everything except our peace of mind. Never be discouraged when faced with obstacles. When you feel downhearted, cheer yourself up and move on wisely and with determination.

15 June 2007

CONFRONTING OBSTACLES
XVIII

Mental Strength

We are here in this present life to perform good deeds. Please maximize your time and effort for this purpose. The flight of life is short, and it is often over much too soon. Do not allow your determination to diminish. Do not be weak-willed, always relying on encouragement from others. Lacking money is not a big deal, but lacking mental strength is dangerous.

15 July 2001

CONFRONTING OBSTACLES
XIX

Remind Yourself

Our mind is full of willpower and it is up to us how much of it we wish to utilize. The amount of willpower in our mind is immense; it is larger than the Himalayas and greater than all the oceans. We should always remind ourselves that the extent of our willpower is boundless and do not be afraid to draw on it. Do not be discouraged and do not retreat because these poor habits will carry on into your future lifetimes.

15 July 2001

CONFRONTING
OBSTACLES
XX
Dissolve Discouragement

When we feel discouraged, disconsolation
will flood into our hearts.

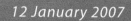
12 January 2007

Simply turn
discouragement into
motivation. You will discover
that the best way to adjust
your thinking is to let go
and reassure yourself with
determination. Keep up
with meritorious deeds and
be confident that you will
definitely receive favorable
outcomes in the future.

CONFRONTING
OBSTACLES
XXI
Endure to Enlighten

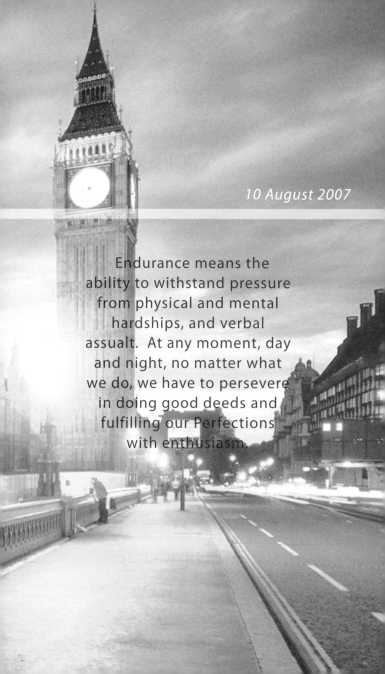

10 August 2007

Endurance means the
ability to withstand pressure
from physical and mental
hardships, and verbal
assualt. At any moment, day
and night, no matter what
we do, we have to persevere
in doing good deeds and
fulfilling our Perfections
with enthusiasm.

CONFRONTING OBSTACLES XXII

Fight for Success

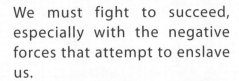

We must fight to succeed, especially with the negative forces that attempt to enslave us.

As evil thoughts direct us to commit misdeeds, we receive poor karmic outcomes in return. Since it originates in the mind, we have to fight with it mentally by resisting any temptation that comes across. Just like the *Bodhisattas* (Buddhahood pursuants) of the past, all we need is a strong will to stay focused and steadfast on our goal.

16 October 2004

28 September 2003

SOLUTIONS
FROM WISDOM
XXIII
Meditation is the Source of Wisdom

Problems can be solved by using wisdom gained through meditation, when we reach a state of mental stillness that is clear from all thoughts and worries. Once we stop thinking, we will enjoy serenity and attain wisdom within, leading to wiser solutions while nourishing ourselves with knowledge and pure energy. Eventually, we will discover the solutions to our problems.

SOLUTIONS FROM WISDOM XXIV

Abate the Severe Consequences

When we suffer, just remember the Lord Buddha's teachings and remain calm. We should accept that suffering is a consequence of our wrongdoing in the past. It is the fruit of our own deeds, and we have to fix it ourselves by focusing our mind on doing only good deeds. To make amends, we should frequently give alms, observe the precepts and meditate, as these practices will give us strength, wisdom and courage to deal with problems. In this way, we can reduce or solve our problems.

12 December 2006

SOLUTIONS FROM WISDOM XXV

The Mind as an Origin

Do not be overwhelmed with suffering. Keep your mind at peace in order to maintain equilibrium. The mind is the source of life energy, willpower, wisdom and accumulated merit energy. These are required to confront all crises and mishaps that arise as a result of our past demerits and mistakes.

Since we cannot change the past or undo our mistakes, the only way to make amends with the irreparable past is to make more merits. There is no other way. Only merits can counter the demerits - this is the principle.

26 October 2003

SOLUTIONS FROM WISDOM
XXVI

The Power of Merit

Merit is the most important factor that can lead us to a successful career and life. It will bring us positive thought, courage, and outcomes. All our endeavours will be achieved easily and successfully. We will be surrounded by good colleagues and subordinates who are willing to support us.

*Moreover, the power of our merit
will destine us to live in a good
environment and experience
pleasant events so that we can
continue making more merit.*

13 August 2007

SOLUTIONS FROM WISDOM XXVII

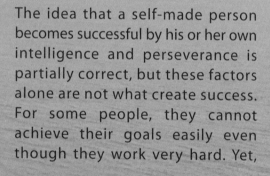

Succeed by Thought

The idea that a self-made person becomes successful by his or her own intelligence and perseverance is partially correct, but these factors alone are not what create success. For some people, they cannot achieve their goals easily even though they work very hard. Yet,

there are others who arrive at success simply by thinking and planning. This is because there are many people eager to help them, turning the situation in their favour. This is the working of their merit, which can be quite fascinating to see.

13 August 2007

Generally, courage and wisdom are already present within us. There is no need to find it elsewhere, but we simply draw it out for personal use by training our mind with positive thinking and self-encouragement.

SOLUTIONS
FROM WISDOM
XXVIII

Courage and Wisdom

2 May 2007

Also, we can boost our morale by accumulating merits from performing as many good deeds as possible. Since we know that our deeds will render good results, we will be more encouraged.

SOLUTIONS FROM WISDOM XXIX

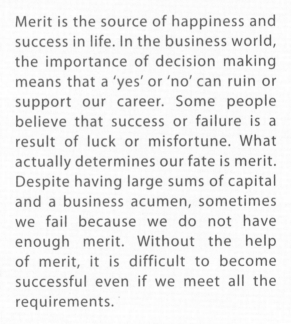

Merit Support

Merit is the source of happiness and success in life. In the business world, the importance of decision making means that a 'yes' or 'no' can ruin or support our career. Some people believe that success or failure is a result of luck or misfortune. What actually determines our fate is merit. Despite having large sums of capital and a business acumen, sometimes we fail because we do not have enough merit. Without the help of merit, it is difficult to become successful even if we meet all the requirements.

1 October 2007

SOLUTIONS FROM WISDOM XXX

More Merit… Less Obstacles

The more merit we have the fewer obstacles we will encounter in life, and vice versa. This is a truth that we should take into consideration. Fortunately, we have a chance to learn the teachings of the Lord Buddha. Therefore, we should accumulate more merit through good deeds because they are the source of our happiness and success.

13 March 2007

SOLUTIONS FROM WISDOM XXXI

Understand Retribution

12 December 2006

Learning the Law of Karma is a must, but this should not make us feel sad, discouraged and hopeless.

Neither should we abandon our lives to desperation or escape from the truth. We study the Law of Karma in order to understand that every single thought, speech, or act, has its effect. Acknowledging this fact, we learn to accept the truth that sufferings are merely karmic consequences.

We must use the knowledge about the Law of Karma to solve the problems in our lives.

First we have to stop and stand firm before taking any action. Drinking alcohol, gambling, or committing suicide to escape is not the right solution. When facing problems, we must clear our mind of all thoughts and anxiety, and recollect the teachings of the Lord Buddha. Keep doing good deeds like sharing, observing the precepts and meditating as a way to improve the situation.

SOLUTIONS
FROM WISDOM
XXXII

Start Over

12 December 2005

SOLUTIONS
FROM WISDOM
XXXIII

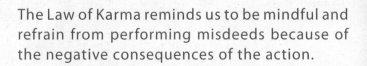

Correlate the Two

The Law of Karma reminds us to be mindful and refrain from performing misdeeds because of the negative consequences of the action.

Unwholesome deeds will lead us to a downfall, or worse, to the realm of suffering, the place of unimaginable torment. As we comprehend this fact, we should restrain and endure in order to overcome obstacles righteously. For whatever problems occur, we have to solve them and move on toward our goal without forgetting to practice meditation in conjunction with merit making.

12 December 2006

SOLUTIONS FROM WISDOM XXXIV

The Four Noble Truths

The Four Noble Truths is an illustration of suffering: its nature, its cause, its cessation and the way leading to cessation. Suffering exists as a result of sensual desires. We are prone to spoiling ourselves and we tend to struggle for acquisition endlessly. Once we realize the cause of suffering, we must learn how to end it. Since the mind is the source of all desires, we must uproot desire from the mind.

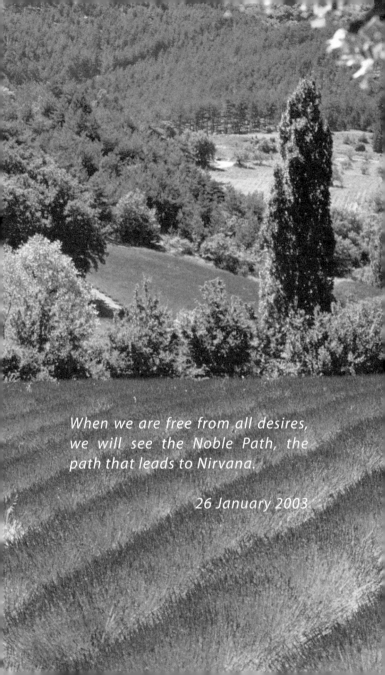

When we are free from all desires, we will see the Noble Path, the path that leads to Nirvana.

26 January 2003

SOLUTIONS FROM WISDOM XXXV

Overcome Suffering

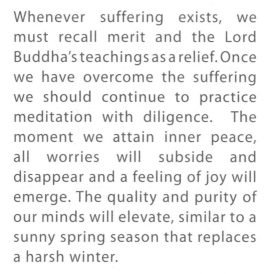

Whenever suffering exists, we must recall merit and the Lord Buddha's teachings as a relief. Once we have overcome the suffering we should continue to practice meditation with diligence. The moment we attain inner peace, all worries will subside and disappear and a feeling of joy will emerge. The quality and purity of our minds will elevate, similar to a sunny spring season that replaces a harsh winter.

30 March 2003

THE WAY OF SOLITUDE

XXXVI

We are What We Think

If we know how to control our thoughts, we can focus our minds on positive things, and in this way, we can enjoy everyday life. Our happiness depends on the way we think. If the mind is obsessed with worry, we will be worried; to be happy is to think of happiness. No one can control our minds except ourselves, and thus, we are given the choice. So, happy or unhappy, it is up to the way we think.

14 September 2004

THE WAY OF SOLITUDE XXXVII

The Mind is Transformable

Let's remove all worries and bad feelings first. Isn't it amazing? If we want to feel sad, we just think sad thoughts, and we begin to feel sad immediately.

If we want to feel good, we just think of a wholesome subject such as the Lord Buddha or the Great Master Phramong-kolthepmuni, the discoverer of Dhammakaya Meditation, as our role models. Or think about pure things like the crystal clear sphere or a Buddha image at the center of our body. If we do so, our mind will become clear and pure as well due to its transformable quality.

5 May 2007

THE WAY OF SOLITUDE
XXXVIII

Do Not Prolong One's Suffering

Suffering remains with us only briefly if we know how to stop prolonging it. Keep yourself from dwelling upon it, and still your mind at the center of your body. Even if you are not able to do much to alleviate your problems at the moment, at least maintain your good spirit.

29 March 2003

THE WAY OF SOLITUDE

XXXIV

Feel Free

5 July 2004

Do not think that you are the only one who suffers. Forget all those bad thoughts and fill yourself with happiness.

Just relax, calm your mind, and focus on the center of your body in search of the inner brightness. Then you will find solutions for the problems and you can liberate yourself from sadness, anxiety, boredom, and other negative feelings.

THE WAY OF SOLITUDE
IVX

Begin with Solitude

To deal with our problems,
we have to collect ourselves first.
The calmness of the mind
will lead us to solutions,
not fear or negative speculation.

We have to admit that what befalls us is a result of our own deeds. When the mind is clear, we can reconsider the cause and effect of the problems more precisely. Learn to forgive those who cause us problems so that our mind is free from anger and vengeance.

THE WAY OF SOLITUDE
IVXI
Immunity of the Mind

The minds of those who do not practice meditation tend to be easily distracted and weakened. This makes them prone to uncontrollable feelings of sadness, stress, boredom, and depression. They are vulnerable because they do not have the immunity to protect their minds from suffering.

6 November 2006

THE WAY OF SOLITUDE

IVXII

Organize Our Thoughts

If our minds are in disarray, we will not be ready for any tasks. Whether we are studying, teaching, or working, a distracted mind will hinder us. Once we learn to concentrate our minds, we can start doing things effectively.

8 June 2007

THE WAY OF SOLITUDE
IVXIII

Make Your Mind Calm and Still

8 July 2007

If you do not know how to deal with the problem, then remove all distracting thoughts from your mind. When the mind is relaxed and calm, you will find the solution. Do not fixate your mind on the complexity of the problem, because powerful wisdom and willpower will only arise from a clear mind.

THE WAY OF
SOLITUDE
IVXIV

The Strength Within

All of us possess the strength within which can be perceived only when our mind is calm. Therefore, no matter how much we suffer, do not lose that calmness. Keep smiling and you will find the solution.

28 February 2006

THE WAY OF SOLITUDE IVXV

The Light of Solitude

When we relax our body and our mind until it reaches a state of stillness, we will find that within that calmness, there is a bright light within our body. At the center of our body there is a path that leads to the cessation of suffering.

10 July 2002

ABOVE ALL CIRCUMSTANCES IVXVI

The Things that Remain

Even if we lose every single thing in our lives, we still have our life and can attain a peaceful mind at the center of our body. If we do not know how to deal with the situation, we can begin with our mind. When the mind is clear, we will have both the wisdom and courage to cope with the problems. Do not worry about the scarcity of material wealth as long as you possess spiritual wealth. Simply meditate and keep your mind positive, and soon you will be better off.

24 November 2006

ABOVE ALL CIRCUMSTANCES
IVXVII
Outward Movement, Inward Stillness

Our career is merely a secondary priority that goes hand in hand with the *Dhamma* - the spiritual lessons which can be practiced during our daily activities. While we are moving, studying, working, or doing anything, we can rest our minds within the center of our body.

4 June 2007

When we can take control of our mind, we will not be overwhelmed with emotion and pain when facing changes or unexpected events. Thus, our mind will not be influenced by suffering, and will become like a cool spot in a hot furnace.

Whenever we recall the Triple Gem - comprising the Buddha, Dhamma, and Sangha - we will be blessed with the power of goodness. This will protect us from all harm, unless it is due to our karmic retribution.

ABOVE ALL CIRCUMSTANCES IVXVIII

Unperturbed by Our Surroundings

This also prepares us for whatever occurrences that may happen. Although death is inevitable and may arrive without warning, we will be unperturbed by the fear and worry about how, where or when we will die. Courage to face death will arise when we attain the inner *Dhamma* through meditation. In addition to peace and joy, we will have loving-kindness and goodwill toward our fellow humankind. Even if our surroundings are constantly changing, our mind will remain unperturbed.

22 June 2007

The insight we gain from meditation is like a boundless knowledge that can provide answers to all our questions. In addition, we can redesign our way of living, beginning with ourselves in pursuit of righteousness and perfection, as well as introducing it to others.

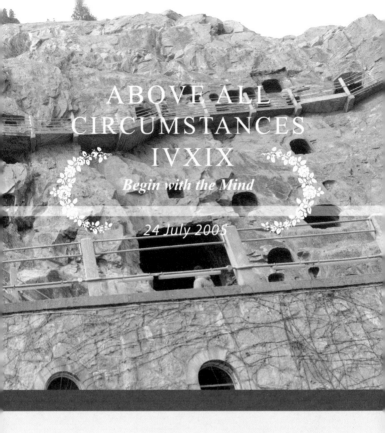

ABOVE ALL CIRCUMSTANCES
IVXIX

Begin with the Mind

24 July 2005

When we can direct our minds to this, it means we are setting the path towards "the revitalization of life." This can be possible only when we achieve mental stillness through meditation.

ABOVE ALL CIRCUMSTANCES VX

The Joyful Heart

Meditation allows us to stay calm and joyful while living amongst various types of people. With a stable mind, we can have a new perspective of the world despite the fact that nothing else has changed. We will become more open-minded to other people. The world will appear to be more cheerful, which can make it easier for us to smile. Like flowers that blossom with the nourishment of water, our minds will blossom with joy with the practice of mediation.

11 December 2005

ABOVE ALL CIRCUMSTANCES
VXI

Peace and Happiness

When our mind is centered
in the middle of our body,
we will experience inner peace and joy.
We can achieve harmony
between the body and mind.
The practice of meditation
will lead to better sleep,
with either non-disturbing dreams
or dreamlessness. When we wake up,
we will feel refreshed as if
emerging from a source of pure energy,
giving us infinite wisdom,
happiness, and willpower.
All of these qualities will exist
with the opening of our eyes.

11 December 2005

ABOVE ALL CIRCUMSTANCES VXII

Stillness is the Key to Success

Sometimes we waste time and energy on problems and stress, which does not solve anything. If we stop struggling with life and meditate, we will find our lives pleasurable and gain utmost satisfaction and true happiness. The mind will be brimming with purity, strength, wisdom, compassion, and loving-kindness for all sentient beings regardless of their nationality, beliefs and race.

8 July 2007

11 December 2005

Once we have attained happiness from meditation, we will feel refreshed and cheerful. Happiness from a pure mind will penetrate through every cell of our body, making us invigorated. Our family and friends will notice the changes and want to be close to us because our joy brings them joy as well.

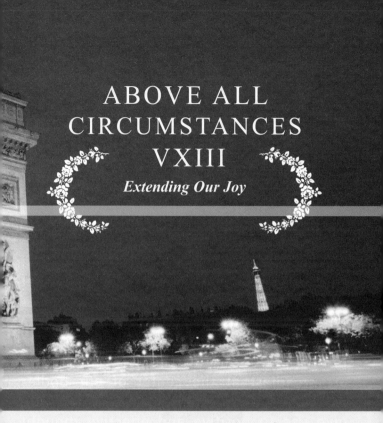

ABOVE ALL CIRCUMSTANCES VXIII

Extending Our Joy

This feeling of happiness will reduce stress and keep our mind from unwholesome thoughts. This will create a pleasant environment at home and in the work place; thus, we will live and work together with less conflict, enabling us to reach our goals together.

ABOVE ALL CIRCUMSTANCES
VXIV

Meditation for Mental Strength

We must practice meditation in order to attain true happiness, which will arise only when we bring our minds back within ourselves. When our minds are still, we will be happy within ourselves and have no need to search for happiness elsewhere. When our minds are steadfast at the center of our bodies, we will gain a wholesome awareness that give rise to positive and effective thought, words and actions. Then our lives will be filled with happiness and success. We will not feel discouraged by problems or obstacles. Meditation will help reduce inner conflicts both within and outside the family. Since our mental strength is sound enough to withstand negativity, we will be mindful to refrain from doing unwholesome deeds.

26 September 2006

ABOVE ALL CIRCUMSTANCES VXV

The Sun Inside

The sun inside of us will glow when our mind is still. Its brightness will radiate all day and night; unlike the sun in the sky which shines only during day. If we attain the sun inside, our lives will never face darkness again. Although we may not always be able to change things the way we want, we will remain unaffected by them because our mind is connected to the inner sun or *Dhamma* sphere that nourishes us with peace and joy.

23 June 2007

THE POWER OF THE MIND VXVI

Elevate Your Motivation

The nature of the mind is capricious. It can be joyful one moment and discontented the next. This is because our mind is contaminated by defilements.

Therefore, it is necessary to seek advice from the teacher-monks or spiritual friends who can motivate us when we feel downhearted. Listening to sermons from monks, witnessing integrity within our spiritual community and following our fellow friends who persevere in meditation practice, will make us more eager to keep up with our meditation and rid ourselves of all defilements.

1 August 2004

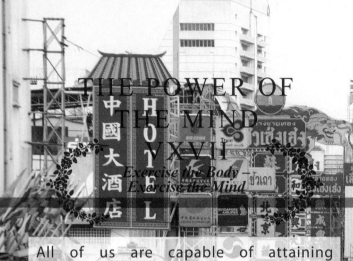

THE POWER OF
THE MIND
VXVII

Exercise the Body –
Exercise the Mind

All of us are capable of attaining *Dhammakaya* - it depends on how much effort we put into practicing meditation. Do not beg for encouragement from anybody because we already possess enormous willpower to drive us towards our goal. Since it can never be exhausted, utilize it as much as possible. Interestingly, both willpower and physical energy actually becomes more powerful the more we resort to them. Therefore, we can gain mental strength by exercising our mind in the same way that we exercise our body to gain physical strength.

14 July 2003

THE POWER OF THE MIND VXVIII

The Ultimate Courage

Meditation energizes us with the willpower to confront our troubles without fear or worry. Our willpower will be recharged automatically by an internal force that enhances courage. We will stay calm and view obstacles as a challenge. Only the goals matter because obstacles are there for us to overcome. Meditation is the key factor leading to uncompromising courage to fight for one's goals. Moreover, people who meditate will also have *Dhamma* and the Lord Buddha as their refuge and blessing for victory.

28 February 2005

10 May 2005

We should always keep in mind that meditation is essential for us, like air for breathing and food for a healthy life. Meditation is food for our mind and will bring about good mental health. It will also protect us against any mental disease.

THE POWER OF THE MIND
VXIX

Meditation is Food for the Mind

We will be happy at all times and able to welcome any challenges with a smile. Whatever else we might lose, our peace of mind will never diminish.

THE POWER OF THE MIND VIX

Meditate Consistently

Despite illness, lack of sleep, heavy workloads and stress, we should always make time for meditation. While meditating, we can rest if we are sleepy, change our position to ease the pain, and open our eyes when we are distracted. There will always be problems in life, but we should continue to meditate since it can lead us to solutions. This is why we should meditate consistently.

25 July 2006

THE POWER OF THE MIND

VIXI

Organize the Mind through Meditation

If we meditate everyday, our minds will be familiar with the center of the body and being in a focused state. This practice does not only refine our minds, it will improve our thoughts, speech and actions and cause us to be more organized, thus helping us to achieve maximum efficiency. Although we may be tempted by worldly pleasures, we will not fall into the traps of demerit, a proof of the strength of our minds.

10 May 2006

THE POWER OF THE MIND VIXII

The Power from Stillness

Regular meditation will result in courage to overcome obstacles and temptations, and eventually we will have control of our own minds. This can be possible if we empower ourselves every single day by stilling the mind. All of us should take this into account.

10 May 2006

THE POWER OF THE MIND
VIXIV

A True Hero

The person who conquers himself is a true hero. The real battlefield is not anywhere in this world, but the world inside us. All the time, we need to fight against greed, anger and delusion which are the roots of all problems that affect us and the whole world. Only the people who bring peace to this world by stilling their minds will deserve to be addressed as a 'hero.'

4 August 2006

ABOVE ALL
CIRCUMSTANCES
VIXIV
One Step Back

In any confrontation, just take one step back from your standing point and it will help resolve conflict. This does not mean that you surrender. We are showing the signs of our maturity by smiling at each other, cooling ourselves down or being more flexible. In order to win we give in. Win what? Win the hearts of other people because when we win over someone's heart, there is no need to argue anymore.

3 April 2006

ABOVE ALL CIRCUMSTANCES
VIXV

Win Their Hearts

The way to win over the hearts of other people who are unkind to us is to learn to forgive and forbear. Similar to chopping sandalwood with an axe, even though an axe is used to cut through the sandalwood harshly, it receives fragrance on its blade in return. Likewise, no matter what others do to hurt us, we should do only good deeds in return, and we will win over their hearts in time. It will be a permanent and sustainable victory which will be rewarded with love and best wishes.

22 June 2006

ABOVE ALL CIRCUMSTANCES VIXVI

The Symbol of Victory

9 November 2003

Whenever you feel weak and discouraged, take a look at The Memorial Hall of The Great Master Phramongkolthepmuni or The Master Nun Chand Khonnokyoong. As the great leaders of our spiritual community, they have no fear of obstacles and never gave up or retreated throughout their lives.

Their memorial halls are symbols of victory that inspire us to become good fighters ourselves. Our courage in the pursuit of perfection will be rejuvenated just like the spirit of soldiers when they notice that their Commander-in-Chief's flag still flutters elegantly.

THE TRUE REFUGE VIXVII

Goal of Life

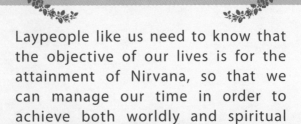

Laypeople like us need to know that the objective of our lives is for the attainment of Nirvana, so that we can manage our time in order to achieve both worldly and spiritual development.

Each morning, after rising from bed, we should chant and meditate to calm the mind in preparation for the day. Before bed, again, it is the time for prayer and meditation which will help to cleanse our mind from the stress and problems we have faced. Then we will have a sound and peaceful sleep.

6 November 2006

THE TRUE REFUGE VIXVIII

Never Retreat… Never Regress

27 January 2002

We should always try to improve our mind. Perseverance is very important. Never retreat, regress or give up even though you feel lazy or careless. Will yourself to meditate everyday until it becomes a habit, and then it will become natural for you to observe your mind at all times. Keep noticing if you are proceeding in the right direction and remember how to focus your mind. Regular practice will lead us to the ultimate refuge, which is the Triple Gem within.

THE TRUE REFUGE
VIXIX

Task for the Mind

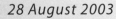

28 August 2003

Do not let your routine practice of meditation be interrupted by any external factors. Meditation is a task for the mind and does not require any physical effort. We only need to visualize a crystal-clear sphere or a crystal-clear Buddha image at the center of our body at all times.

This process is called meditation, or bhavana which is compatible with other physical tasks. Similar to driving, the mind and parts of the body can function together at the same time.

THE TRUE REFUGE

VIIX

The True Refuge

19 February 2004

People, animal companions and material things are not a true refuge. These things are not lasting in nature and are subject to change, and at best, they can only be a temporary refuge. Instead, our true refuge is not subject to change, which means that it possesses the omnipotent characteristics: permanence, blissfulness, and true self. Even things which have lasted millions or billions of years like the sun, the moon and stars cannot be our refuge because they too will eventually disappear altogether, along with those people who believe in the planets. The Lord Buddha investigated throughout and beyond the three realms of existence and discovered that the true and only refuge is the Buddha Gem, *Dhamma* Gem and *Sangha* Gem. These three eternal things, known as the Triple Gem, exist within every human being.

Muk Tawan, Thailand

THE TRUE REFUGE

VIIXI

The Chance and the Choice

Disease causes pain and
takes away our health and
strength. In our lives we may
lose anything for any reason,
but as long as our breath and
the light at the center of the
body still remain,
we will be able to use them
to reach our inner peace and
true happiness within.

20 June 2006

THE TRUE REFUGE
VIIXII
Extinguishing Suffering

When we attain the *Dhammakaya* within, there will be no more suffering, boredom, stress, tension, sadness, or grief.

Before attaining *Dhammakaya*, life is like running against the wind with a burning torch in our hand. The flame blowing towards us brings us heat and pain. When we reach a pond and dip the torch into the water, the flame is put out. The coolness of the water replaces the heat and puts an end to our pain. We will soon forget that we were suffering just a short while ago. That is how those who attain the *Dhammakaya* feel. They will feel happy and peaceful, and ready to perform only good deeds. Even in hard times, there will be no loss of courage.

21 May 2004

THE TRUE REFUGE

VIIXIII

Ending Problems

27 September 2007

The seventh base, which is at the center of our body, is the place where all problems end. When the *Dhamma* is reached, all problems cease because the mind finds the answers for itself.

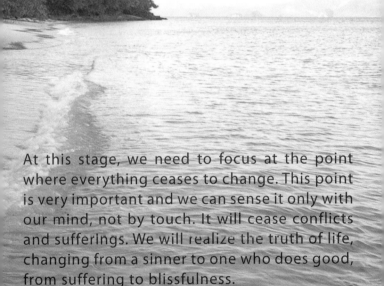

At this stage, we need to focus at the point where everything ceases to change. This point is very important and we can sense it only with our mind, not by touch. It will cease conflicts and sufferings. We will realize the truth of life, changing from a sinner to one who does good, from suffering to blissfulness.

THE TRUE REFUGE VIIXIV

Be Yourself

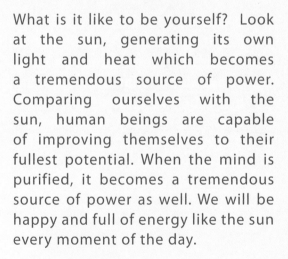

What is it like to be yourself? Look at the sun, generating its own light and heat which becomes a tremendous source of power. Comparing ourselves with the sun, human beings are capable of improving themselves to their fullest potential. When the mind is purified, it becomes a tremendous source of power as well. We will be happy and full of energy like the sun every moment of the day.

11 June 2005

THE TRUE
REFUGE
VIIXV

The Brightness of the Sun

It can be said that no one prefers a life in darkness to a life with a bright future. Sometimes it is unavoidable that darkness comes into our lives, however, we know that when tomorrow comes, all darkness will disappear. With the presence of daylight, we will gain hope and courage.

The light of the day will make things appear more vividly to us, so we are not frightened by what we cannot see. We can make the sun rise at night as well. Just focus the mind at the center of our body until the light glows within. When this inner sun rises at the center of our body, we will feel even happier than when we see the sun of the day.

THE TRUE
REFUGE
VIIXVI

Like the Sun

Whether you live alone
or with other people,
there will always be problems.
There are problems everywhere.

However, we can deal with those problems with wisdom and courage which are derived from the perfection of the mind when we meditate. With this state of mind, we will be like the sun that sheds light on the world every morning. Do not give up meditating. Put your mind at the center of the body all the time, and you will be happy and bright like the sun that provides light and warmth to all living things.

THE TRUE REFUGE VIIXVII

Giving Courage to Others

Before we can encourage other people, we should be able to encourage ourselves first. The only way to empower the mind is to rely on the absolute power of the Triple Gem. If our minds can become one with the power of the Triple Gem, we can make a wish for both ourselves and other people. This is the right way to encourage people.

11 August 2003

THE TRUE REFUGE

VIIXVIII

As You Wish

11 July 2006

By encouraging people to do good deeds, the result will be firmness of the mind. The mind will be strong and filled with unshakable courage. Also, the person will be adorable to all celestial beings and humankind. While meditating, it will be easier to attain Nirvana.

THE TRUE
REFUGE
VIIXIX

Expand Your Mind

Our lifespan is so short while our great destination is far. Hence, we have limited time for performing good deeds and reaching our goal. Do not allow your vision to be narrowed but keep it wide. Envision the whole world in your hands. With determination, everything will fall into place.

7 October 2007

ธรรมกาย
(DHAMMAKAYA)

..., which can be attained by stilling the mind at center of this body, the 7th Base.

THE TRUE REFUGE VIIIX

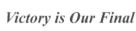

Victory is Our Final

No matter how far we are from our goal, we are never lost. Despite the dim hope of success at times, there is always the possibility of winning. Only determination will lead us to our goal. Although the goal is far and it seems like we are going to lose, if we take the right path and try hard enough we will eventually succeed.

7 October 2007

THE TRUE REFUGE
VIIIXI

A Definite Victory

The absolute goal of attaining *Dhamma* is not easy. Although the middle path is direct, it is immeasurably long. But however long it may be, we will fight and eventually achieve our goal. One knows that righteousness will overcome evil. We must keep making merits as much as possible because when our hearts reach perfection, we will defeat the dark side of our hearts. When the mind is set, it is possible to achieve the goal. There is nothing beyond our reach if we are really determined.

14 September 2007

ing.

ABOUT THE AUTHOR

LUANG POR
DHAMMAJAYO

b. 1944

Luang Por Dhammajayo is the abbot of Dhammakaya Temple and the president of the Dhammakaya Foundation in Thailand. He was born Chaibul Sutthipol on the 22 April 1944. During his adolescence, he became an ardent student at the Meditation Center of Wat Paknam Bhasicharoen where he first met his mentor and spiritual guardian, the Buddhist nun Khun Yay Archaraya (Master

Nun Chand Khonnokyoong). She was one of the most respected Buddhist Meditation teachers at that time. Later on, Chaibul was ordained at Wat Paknam Bhasicharoen on the 27 August 1969. After six years of monkhood, Venerable Dhammajayo became a teacher in the specialized method of meditation known as the Dhammakaya School of meditation founded by Phramongkolthepmuni (The Most Venerable Sodh Candasaro), the great abbot of Wat Paknam Bhasicharoen.

Venerable Dhammajayo himself, is a vital force in the inspiration and teaching of higher meditation and insight. He has succeeded in establishing a model temple which is a prototype of a temple with good discipline, practices, cleanliness, orderliness and holiness, which not only is the model temple accepted nationwide but has also successfully expanded to many countries worldwide. He has also succeeded in establishing a Buddhist satellite network with a 24 hour-a-day broadcasts to effectively expand the Dhamma and meditation teachings to the audience both nationwide and worldwide.

BASIC DHAMMAKAYA MEDITATION

by
Luang Por Dhammajayo

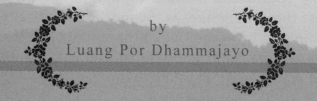

Start by adjusting your sitting position. If you sit on the floor, sit cross-legged, right leg over the left leg, right hand over the left hand, palms up, your right index finger gently touching your left thumb. Place both hands on your lap comfortably, your head and back erect. If you feel uncomfortable in this position, you may sit on a chair or sofa. Adjust your position until you feel completely comfortable, so that the blood will circulate freely, and you breathe naturally.

Gently close your eyes, comfortably, as if you were going to sleep. Do not squeeze your eyelids, do not force them shut. Close them slightly. Do not close them tightly. Sit with a smile on your face. Next, take a deep breath. Inhale and exhale a few times. Breathe in deeply until you feel the air pass through your lungs and reach the middle of your abdomen, and slowly breathe out, through your nostrils. When you breathe in, imagine that each cell in your body is fully taking in the feeling of happiness and joyfulness, and when you breathe out, breathe out all your worries, and negative feelings. Take a moment to let go of all responsibilities that relate to work, loved ones, family, studies, or anything else.

Let everything go. Let your mind be joyful, relaxed, and free from all worry. Then breathe normally. Relax every muscle in your body. Start to relax from the top of your head, down to your forehead. Relax the muscles in your face, your eyelids, your neck, and the muscles in your shoulders, your arms, down to the tips of your fingers. Relax the muscles of your back, your chest, your legs, down to the tips of your toes. Let every part of your body relax. Don't let any part of your body contract, tighten or become tense.

Continue to relax until you feel that every part of your body and each cell in your body are completely relaxed. You are now in a state of complete relaxation, so that you can feel an emptiness, transparency, and lightness. Now, make your mind joyful, cheerful, clear, pure and bright. Release, and let go. Empty your mind.

Make your mind clear, pure, and free from all thoughts. Imagine you are sitting alone in a vast, open space, full of freedom and peacefulness as if you never had any attachment in life, never had any problem, and never known anyone before. Then imagine that your body has no organs, suppose it is a tube, a hole, a hollow, like an inflated balloon, or like a crystal or diamond cylinder, bright and clear. Let it be an open space, empty, hollow inside. You may feel your body get lighter and lighter, as if it is weightless; gradually melting away and becoming one with nature.

Let yourself enjoy this feeling of peacefulness. Now, bring your mind to focus to the center of the body, in the middle of your abdomen, two finger's width above the navel level. If you are a new practitioner, do not worry too much about the exact point of the center of the body; simply maintain your mind, softly, and gently, in the middle of your abdomen. The way that you focus your mind at the center of the body, is by comparing it to the lightness, and gentleness of a bird's feather, that is floating down from the sky and touching the calm surface of the water.

You may feel the soft touch of a bird's feather when it touches the surface of the water. Focus your mind at the center of the body with this feeling. Maintain the feeling of relaxation of your body and mind continuously, while you focus your mind at the center of the body in the middle of your abdomen. After you've found the starting point to focus your mind, softly imagine the meditation object within you, so that the mind can have something on which to focus, and so that your mind will not wander. You can imagine the sun, of any size that you like. Let it be round as a clear pure crystal ball, and bright.

To imagine this object, you need to know the method. Slowly imagine the object, with ease. Relax. Keep it simple, as you might think of a football, a tennis ball, a ping pong ball, or anything that is familiar. Do not force your mind to think of the object to the point that it makes you feel tense. Do not use too much effort. Or else, you will stare at it; that is the wrong method. Gently imagine the object, and relax. It does not matter if it is not clear. Be satisfied with however clear it is. And maintain your mind calmly, let it stop and be still. Think of the bright sun continuously. Do not let your mind wander. If you do think of something else, maintain your mind by repeating the mantra.

Repeat the mantra in your mind softly, as if the soft sound were coming from the center of the sun, in the middle of your abdomen. Repeat the mantra, "Samma Arahang, Samma Arahang, Samma Arahang", which means: purify your mind. So that you will be free from the suffering of life, or you can use any words, such as "clear and bright, clear and bright, clear and bright". Repeat the mantra continuously, while at the same time thinking of the bright sun, gently and comfortably. Focus your mind and be still at the center of pure brightness. Maintain your mind by imagining a bright object, and at the same time repeat the mantra continuously, softly, comfortably, until your mind is still.

Once your mind is completely still, it will drop the words, "Samma Arahang" or "clear and bright" by itself, as if you are forgetting to repeat this mantra, or feel that you don't want to repeat the mantra anymore; or just want to be still, and the mind is not wandering or thinking about anything, and there is only the picture of bright sun appearing clearly at the center of the body. If you feel like this, you do not have to go back to repeating the mantra again. Let your awareness maintain the vision of a bright sun, gently and comfortably. Only do this from this point onward, with a still mind, softly, gently, constantly, continuously. And do not do anything beyond this.

If you have any experience from within, which is different from your meditation object, do not be excited. Let your mind be neutral, as if you had a lot of previous experience in life; observe the experiences that occur with calm mind, relax. Do not question, how this is happening. Just observe, only observing, otherwise your mind will move from the center of the body, and your inner experience will disappear. Observe it with calm mind, be neutral, soon your mind will be completely focused, pure, still, feeling nothingness; this moment is very important, so do not neglect it, pay attention; because the experience from within will progress; your mind should remain only in this state. Your role at this time is to be an observer, just keep observing, keep observing, just relax. Do not think of anything. Do all of this, only this, that is all.

Directions to Wat Phra Dhammakaya, Pathum Thani Province in Thailand

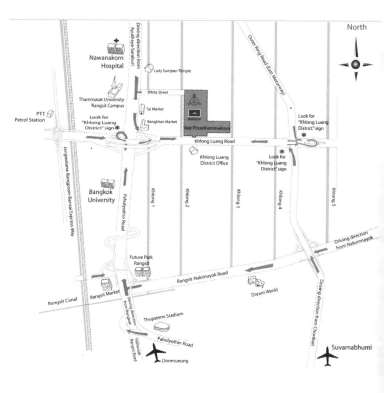

If you do this correctly, easily, comfortably, then your mind will become still easily, effortlessly. If you were an analyst, you would analyze, comment, on your inner experiences, your mind would not be calm, your good experience, would go away. So, just adhere only to my instruction. Eventually, your mind will be refined, and completely focused at the center of the body, and the mind will lead within, entering into clarify, purity, brightness, true happiness , and true inner knowledge , which is the wisdom from within, that lies deeper and deeper, And you will attain that which is in you, that is universal, the same for everyone in this world.